HANNA K. BROJAN

Letters to Myself

First published by Independently published 2024

Copyright © 2024 by Hanna K. Brojan

All rights reserved. No part of this publication may be reproduced, stored or transmitted in any form or by any means, electronic, mechanical, photocopying, recording, scanning, or otherwise without written permission from the publisher. It is illegal to copy this book, post it to a website, or distribute it by any other means without permission.

Hanna K. Brojan asserts the moral right to be identified as the author of this work.

However, the publisher grants permission to take a photo of a few pages from the book for advertising purposes, provided that proper attribution is given and the use is in compliance with applicable copyright laws. Hanna K. Brojan asserts the moral right to be identified as the author of this work.

First edition, 200 copies
Edited by: Hanna K. Brojan
Sharia review: Tarik E. Džaferović
Graphic design: Hanna K. Brojan
Cover design: Maja Aragun (@studiom.fine.art)

Price:

First edition

ISBN: 9798326398529

Cover art by Maja Aragun
Proofreading by Tarik E. Džaferović

This book was professionally typeset on Reedsy.
Find out more at reedsy.com

for everyone striving to get closer to Allah

Contents

Preface x
Acknowledgement xii

I GUIDANCE

privilege and mercy of being a Muslim 3
dependence on Allah's guidance 4
finding the strength 5
searching for meaning 7
newfound life 9
internal battles 10
discovery of islam 11
seeking Allah's guidance and relying on His wisdom 12
purposeful selection 13
ultimate victory despite any efforts to undermine it 14
a journey with its ups and downs 15
Allah's approval 16

II KNOWLEDGE

knowledge of Islam fosters a sense of connection and love... 19
valuable lessons 20

the importance of prioritizing meaningful pursuits	21
understanding the wisdom behind His guidance	22
limited understanding and knowledge about the world	24
deeper understanding	25
appreciate the blessings	26
misrepresentation and unfair labeling	27

III   RELATIONSHIP WITH ALLAH

strengthening the bond with Allah	31
deep sense of sorrow	32
surrendering to the will of Allah, finding the peace in...	33
protection	34
Allah's ultimate control and authority over all matters	35
our ultimate responsibility lies with Allah	36
prioritize Allah's pleasure over the opinions of others	37
Allah is the ultimate source of our needs	38
fear Allah rather than being consumed by fear of other...	39
the importance of remembering Allah	40
unwavering resilience and protection	41
inherent connection between human beings and Allah	42
the immense power and control Allah has over all things	43
the comfort and solace in communication with Allah	44

the importance of seeking guidance through prayer	45
unique perspective on coping with pain	46
humility	47
intentions known to Allah	48
fulfilling connection	49
Islam is a foundation for inner peace	50
relying on Allah	51
healing	52
ultimate authority	53
true closeness	54
deep appreciation	55
importance of humility and gratitude	56
God's unconditional love	57
the more you give	58
my wish for you	59
the true value of faith	60
balance	61
embody this balance	62

IV CLOSE ONES

power and importance of forgiveness	65
rare and precious blessings in life	66
understand that people can come into our lives for specific...	67
don't rely solely on human relationships	68
reality of kindness	69
prioritizing our faith over worldly relationships	70
be bestowed with even greater blessings	71

the transient nature of human relationships
and the... 72
meaningful relationships 74
care and support 75

V MUSLIMAH

clouded judgment 79
personal transformation 80
defending the choice to wear a hijab 81
significant encounter with a woman wearing a hijab, the... 82
deep emotional impact 84
finding liberation within the Islamic faith 85
the positive aspects of hijab 86
journey of wearing a hijab 87
don't compromise our values for acceptance 88
importance of modesty 89
inner qualities and meaningful connections 90
proper hijab 91
freedom 93

VI TRUST

seeking His pleasure 97
the value of embracing sabr 98
personal empowerment and trust in Allah's plan 99
find comfort in Allah's knowledge and understanding 100
even in difficult times, there are blessings
to be found 101

seek solace in prayer and trust Allah during difficult times	102
redirect your prayers towards seeking what is ultimately...	103
level of trust we place in Allah	104
rejections as a form of divine protection	105
Allah never leaves us empty-handed	106
a positive outlook	107
profound and beautiful outcome	108
limitless power and certainty that Alllah possesses	109
importance of obedience	110
surrender and acceptance of reality	111
tawakkul	112
perfect timing	113
surrendering to His plans	114

VII HARAM

it is not worth the damage	117
a result of engaging in haram relationship	118
consequences	119
break free	120
prohibition serves as a means of protection	122
burden	124
remorse and guilt	125
the significance of striving for righteousness	126
impact of sins	127
Allah's judgment	128
regret	129
the consequences of engaging in haram actions and the...	130

longing and vulnerability; surrender and emotional turmoil	131
tranquility	132
manipulating the boundaries of halal	133
self-control and discipline	134
the long-term consequences	135
genuine concern	136
staying true to the teachings of the faith	137
protective shield	138
stay alert	139
heartfelt prayer	140
remorse	141
priorities	142
the void within one's soul	143

VIII REPENTANCE

pure hearts	147
repentance becomes a lifeline	148
emotional aftermath	149
clash between the shame and guilt	150
recognizing one's worth and avoiding self-pity	151
the tendency of humanity to be impatient and seek immediate...	152
the mercy and forgiveness of Allah	153
satan's deceitful whispers and manipulative intentions	154
let go	155
plea for forgiveness	156
shortcomings in repentance	158
virtue of forgiveness	159

IX CHANGE

depth of commitment to my faith	163
it is okay	164
freedom to change	165
Allah does not hold your past against you	166
focus on the present and future rather than dwelling on the...	167
the tendency to modify our behavior based on who is...	168
find a hidden message in this one	169
challenges faced by reverts	170
hope and encouragement	171
growth and development	172
the power of prayer	173
new perspective	174
responsibilities	175
powerful	176
grow	177

X GRATITUDE

pause and engage in a moment, express gratitude	181
gratitude and humility before Allah	182
positive transformation	183
generosity and selflessness	184
power of gratitude	185
kept between oneself and Allah	186
balanced mindset	187
seemingly minor actions may hold great value	188
the ultimate source of everything	189

XI HEREAFTER

detachment	193
making the most of each moment	194
true fulfillment lie in the hereafter	196
crucial decisions	197
confront the topic of death and be mindful of it	198
the temporary attractions of this worldly life	199
importance of effort	200
striving for excellence in one's actions and deeds	201
the fleeting nature of worldly desires and everlasting joy...	202
never ultimately defeated	203
pursuing worldly perfection is ultimately futile, as it is...	204
worldly pursuits and possession	205
profound admiration and love	206
rewards promised in Jannah	207
preserve and find strength	208
longing	209
appreciation for the present moment	210
the trap of procrastination and underestimation of the...	211
the importance of continuous self-improvement	212
deep concern for your non-Muslim family members	213
no way to escape	214
wise choices	215
keep your focus on what is eternal and of greater...	216
focus where it matters	217
charity	218

be mindful	219
forgetful species are we	220
AFTERWORD	221

Preface

Letters to Myself

BISMILLAH!

Esselam alaikum brothers and sisters,

I'm excited to share something special with you - my thoughts and feelings all bundled up in "Letters to Myself." Why that title? Well, these words were first for me, a personal journey. Now, I want to share them with you in the hope that they bring something good to your life.

This little book talks about 11 important things. Like how Allah guides us, what I've learned about Islam, and the ties we have with our family and friends. We'll chat about being a Muslimah, what trust in Allah means, making up for mistakes, why change is okay, and why saying "thank you" to Allah matters a lot.

I also share some thoughts about tricky stuff like wrong relationships and big no-nos. The book is like a friendly guide, helping us understand these things better.

So, let's journey together through these pages. They're not

a rulebook, just a friendly chat about life and faith. I hope it brings you some joy and makes you feel a bit closer to Allah.

With lots of good wishes and prayers,

Hanna K. Brojan
  May, 2024

May Allah shower His mercy upon you and guide you on this journey of understanding and faith. May these words be a source of enlightenment and draw you closer to Him. Ameen.

Acknowledgement

A heartfelt thank you to my loved ones who supported me when I decided to write this book.

Special gratitude to my husband, my unwavering support and rock.

Thanks a bunch to Mirela, always ready to lend a helping hand with a cheerful heart.

A sincere acknowledgement to Tarik for his significant contribution to the Sharia review.

A warm appreciation to Maja (@studiom.fine.art) for crafting the most beautiful cover in the world and offering unwavering support and kind words.

A big shoutout to Merdijja for the heartfelt review, your honesty, and appreciation. You're truly one of a kind.

Finally, a big thank you to every reader holding this book, prepared to connect with me through my words. I appreciate the chance to share and, inshAllah, help you draw nearer to our Creator.

I

GUIDANCE

hidayah / istikhara / salat

In this chapter of the book, the verses beautifully express the idea of seeking guidance from Allah, portraying it as a guiding light that helps believers navigate their spiritual journey.

privilege and mercy of being a Muslim

Being a Muslim is indeed a privilege and Allah's boundless mercy. Among countless individuals Allah chose YOU and guided you to the righteous path, this blessing should never be taken for granted. You can be on the Right path now, but this can change in the blink of an eye.

let the awareness of this privilege serve as a reminder to cherish and protect your faith, for its value cannot be overstated.

dependence on Allah's guidance

Guide us
ya Rabb.
Guidance is
what we need.

finding the strength

I've been judged before people saw & met me,
judged before they even knew my name.
They deemed me unworthy,
assuming the worst,
fabricating stories about me,
their twisted minds were jealous of me.

They thought it would shatter my pride & feelings,
believing it would tear me apart.

I crumbled, losing myself,
there was a moment when I gasped for breath
but I couldn't end it, not like that.
There was so much more I had to give &
God decided that I shall live.

Ever since, I've battled against myself, for myself.
No one tells you this in youth,
your greatest adversary is the one…
the one you see in the mirror's reflection.

I emerged victorious from the fight within,

I conquered my worst enemy,
now they may try to break me,
but since I've tasted the pain of being shattered,
I'll only wish them good luck in their futile attempts.

searching for meaning

In my younger years,
I would often weep myself to sleep,
asking God for guidance
otherwise I'll trip.

Years have come and gone,
as I plummeted into despair,
and in the depths,
in the darkest corners of my being,
…
I discovered it there.

I had to reach my lowest point,
to find what was truly the best for me.

It was Allah
showing me the path.

He was there when I reached my worst
because He knew that's when I would
need Him the most.

the quote underscores the transformative power of reaching a low point and finding guidance and strength in the relationship with Allah. It serves as a reminder that even in our darkest moments, Allah is always there, ready to lead us towards the path that is best for us.

newfound life

They still hope that this is just a phase
and that the old me will come back.
What they do not know is
that I am truly alive because
Allah bestowed Islam upon me,
and reignited my will to
exist and thrive.

internal battles

The old me is never coming back.
The old me remains in the past.

If only they knew the battles I waged
with the old me,
they would never inquire of me
"Where is she?"

discovery of islam

I was unaware of different path
before Islam.
I was oblivious to the true essence
of genuine happiness.
Happiness that doesn't lie in
misguided pursuits..

Through Islam, Allah revealed to us
the way of finding tranquility solely in Him.

It was always Him, only Him.

He became the sole route to happiness and serenity,
the nearer I draw,
the greater my heart finds contentment.

It was always Him,
only Him.

seeking Allah's guidance and relying on His wisdom

Before making a decision,
ask Allah for guidance.

After making a decision,
put your trust in Allah.

purposeful selection

You were chosen among so many.
You were always meant to be a Muslim.
It's your biggest blessing.

Be thankful every single day.

You
were
chosen.

ultimate victory despite any efforts to undermine it

Islam finds its way into people's hearts,
no matter how hard many try to blacken it.

They can try,
but they're never gonna defeat us.

Muslims are holding Islam so closely
to their hearts
that no army of humankind
can defeat it.

Allahu Akbar – God is Most Great

a journey with its ups and downs

I miss the times when I first converted to Islam.
It feels like that was when I put in the most effort to learn about Islam, prayed more, and was more focused.
I was a better version of myself than I am today,
and I want to regain that.

Allah's approval

When in doubt, uncertain which way to go…
always choose the one you know Allah will approve.

II

KNOWLEDGE

'ilm / iqra' / tahqiq
The verses in this section serve as a poetic tribute to
the significance of knowledge in Islamic teachings,
encouraging individuals to seek wisdom and
enlightenment through study and reflection.

knowledge of Islam fosters a sense of connection and love for Allah

The more knowledge you have
about Islam and our Creator
the easier it becomes to
obey His orders.

by acquiring knowledge about Islam, individuals gain a deeper understanding of its teachings, values, and wisdom. this understanding helps them comprehend the significance and reasoning behind Allah's commands, making it easier for them to align their actions with His will.

valuable lessons

Sulaiman, alaihis salam, beautifully said:
"My Lord, enable me to be grateful for Your favor which You have bestowed upon me and upon my parents and to do righteousness of which You approve. And admit me by Your mercy into {the ranks of} Your righteous servants." Qur'an 27:19

What you can learn from that is:
- give thanks for the blessings that Allah has bestowed upon you
- do good deeds that Allah loves so you can earn His pleasure with you
- you should strive to be the best version of yourself so Allah will join you with the righteous among His servants.

the importance of prioritizing meaningful pursuits

Do not waste your precious time on trivial and insignificant matters in this Dunya (of this world).
Instead, invest your time in acquiring knowledge about Islam – learn and grow – dedicate your free time to the study of the Qur'an and engage in remembrance of Allah – dhikr, pray every Sunnah prayer. Through these actions build a strong bond with your Creator.

This is true happiness,
this is what will calm your heart and soul.

understanding the wisdom behind His guidance

Allah told us to refrain from taking non-Muslims as close friends.

At times, I wondered why,
as some appear genuinely good and kind.

But when you try to think about it
and go deeper,
you realize that
there's something missing,
there's something we don't know,
and there's something we don't see.

Only Allah perceives what lies within,
and He decided that they
guided will not be.

Allah holds knowledge beyond our reach.

And this is why now I always think twice
who and how much to trust

if they're not Muslims,
even if they're family.

limited understanding and knowledge about the world

We are sometimes
walking on this Earth
like we 'know it all'
when in reality
we know nothing at all.

deeper understanding

Never ever stop learning
about Islam.
The more knowledge you acquire,
the easier it becomes...

...to stay away from haram.

appreciate the blessings

When you're trying to improve yourself,
seek advice from people who are 'above' you
and has more knowledge and faith than you.

And always try to stay humble,
look at those below you
so you cannot belittle
the favors of Allah.

misrepresentation and unfair labeling

Islam teaches us to stay away from
  - anger
  - lust
  - ego
  - hatred
  - stubbornness
  - arrogance
  - ignorance
  - narcissism
  - hypocrisy
  - dishonesty
  - violence
  - envy
  - selfishness

yet despite these teachings, there are still attempts to portray us
as the bad guys…

III

RELATIONSHIP WITH ALLAH

taqwa / ibadah / sabr

These poems dive into the profound and intimate bonds people develop in their spiritual journey, strengthening their relationship with Allah.

strengthening the bond with Allah

Rather than focusing on your love life
prioritize your relationship with your Creator.
Focus on getting to know Him better,
focus on getting closer with Him
and focus on building an indestructible bond with Him.

Because wAllahi this is the only
relationship in your life
that will bring you
no harm,
only
joy
&
happiness.

deep sense of sorrow

How heart-wrenching it is
for me to witness
muslims
drifting away from islam.

My heart shatters,
when they neglect a salah,
tucking it away in the recesses of their mind.

Come back!
Come back!
Come back!

surrendering to the will of Allah, finding the peace in fulfilling His commandments

I'm so tired of everything sometimes,
tired of always being something to someone,
when in reality I just want to be nobody to everyone.
I simply want to be the servant of Allah, and that's enough.

protection

Allah showed me a way
and bestowed upon me the tools
to combat and triumph over my own battles.

My weapon consists of
5 daily prayers, dhikr & the Qur'an.
Every day of my life,
they rescue me from myself
and help me to stay sane.

Allah's ultimate control and authority over all matters

I know you've probably heard this many times
- if Allah wills it'll happen -
and I know it's hard to believe it sometimes.

While waiting for it to happen
work on & build up your relationship
with our Creator.
The closer you are to Him, the easier it gets to believe.

our ultimate responsibility lies with Allah

You don't owe anyone anything,
except Allah.
To Him you owe everything.

prioritize Allah's pleasure over the opinions of others

If you're constantly preoccupied
with what others will think,
you'll sink.

But if you only care about Allah
and if He's pleased,
you'll win.

Allah is the ultimate source of our needs

Realize once and for all
that it is Allah you truly need.
It is only Him,
no one else.

fear Allah rather than being consumed by fear of other people

Allah instructed us to not fear people
but to fear Him alone.
Don't fear the creation,
fear the Creator.

Why do we so frequently find ourselves
doing the contrary?

the importance of remembering Allah

He, the Most High, said:
"remember Me; I will remember you…" Qur'an 2:152

Yet, why is He then the last one
to occupy our thoughts?

unwavering resilience and protection

If Allah is your
source of strength,
nothing & no one
can break you.

inherent connection between human beings and Allah

We always belonged to Him,
that's why our hearts are full
when close to Him.

the immense power and control Allah has over all things

Once I realized that
indeed
everything is in
His power,
I stopped fighting
and left it all to Him.
I'm not regretting it.

the comfort and solace in communication with Allah

Even though I know
He knows
already,
I still find peace
& ease
when telling
Him
everything.

the importance of seeking guidance through prayer

When life gets too hard,
I only find comfort
in conversation
with Him.

unique perspective on coping with pain

How am I coping with pain?
I am learning to love it.
Yes, that may be strange…
Why would anyone want to love the pain?

I'll tell you a secret
but promise you won't tell…

Pain pushes me closer to Allah.
The higher the pain, the closer I get.

Maybe, after all, it is not the pain I love,
but what comes with and after it.

humility

Even if you think
you're in charge
of your life,
you're really not.

Let's stay humble,
shall we?

intentions known to Allah

People don't need to know
what your intentions are
because Allah already does.

fulfilling connection

Taking solitude
with one self and
relying on Him alone
is more than enough.

Islam is a foundation for inner peace

Life with Islam is so peaceful,
even the situations that would
usually stress you out, become easy to bear…

relying on Allah

Sometimes you're left with nothing,
so you can turn to Allah
and realize He's the only One
who's always there.

You're left with nothing
to gain everything.

healing

Purify your heart often.
Best therapy I ever had
was crying
out loud
on sajdah.

ultimate authority

It's funny how people still believe in luck
while it has always been Allah.
He gives and He takes as He wishes.

true closeness

Choosing to obey Allah
rather than following your own desires
is what will bring you closer to Him.

deep appreciation

My Beloved Servant.

His words
that can cure our
broken hearts.

importance of humility and gratitude

Allah has no need for your worship,
it's you who needs Him,
not the other way around.

God's unconditional love

All my life, I was searching for unconditional love;
For someone who would love me, regardless of my mistakes, regardless of my shortcomings, regardless of my imperfections…

Unknowingly, I was seeking something that only God can provide.

His love for you is and will remain unconditional.
You can sin, repent, sin again, and repent some more.
He will welcome you back every single time.
No one else can do that
except Him.
You can mess up 100 times,
and repent 101 times,
and He'll let you come back,
won't cease to love you,
won't abandon you…

Only God
can bestow this type of love,
only God!

the more you give

When we put Allah first,
the whole Dunya (world) starts chasing us.

Allah never leaves us empty-handed,
the more we give, the more we receive.

my wish for you

I wish for you
many
sleepless nights.

I wish for you
many
lonely nights.

I wish
you would cry.

Cry out to your Creator,
alone, when everyone else is sleeping but you,
working on strengthening your relationship with Allah.

I wish all of that
from the bottom
of my heart.

the true value of faith

Even if to the external world it may appear that you're not living the most lavish life because you're abstaining from some of the worldly pleasures, you are, in fact, on the winning side. You might not be the wealthiest, the most beautiful, or the most intelligent, but you are a Muslim, and that's your most valuable attribute.

True faith, walking the righteous path, is more valuable than anything in this worldly life. You already possess everything you need! Don't ever believe that lacking the "best" in this world diminishes your value in the eyes of Allah.

If Allah has guided you, if He loves you, you are among the most prosperous ones!

balance

Life is about finding the middle path.
You need to push yourself,
but not excessively.
At times you might need to ease up,
but not too much.
You will occasionally stumble,
make errors,
and face judgment from others,
but remember Allah doesn't judge you in the same way.
So, keep moving forward.

embody this balance

Even though Allah loves strong believers,
don't forget to keep your heart soft.

Maintaining a soft heart
while being strong in faith and character
is highly regarded in Islam.

IV

CLOSE ONES

Silat al-Rahim / wali / ukhuwwah

In this chapter, the verses beautifully illuminate the importance of close friends and family bonds in Islam, portraying them as a cherished gift from Allah.

power and importance of forgiveness

Being able to forgive
those who have wronged you
is truly a gift.

rare and precious blessings in life

It's rare to find friends who will
celebrate your wins,
cry for your losses,
support you on your way up,
listen to you when you are unable to talk.
It's rare to find friends who will
remind you of your Lord,
take your hand and urge you towards goodness.
It's rare to find friends like that,
and if you ever get lucky enough,
hold onto them
and thank Allah.

understand that people can come into our lives for specific reasons and depart once their purpose has been fulfilled

If Allah guided you to the right path through someone you know, it does not necessarily mean that this person will stay in your life forever.
Sometimes in life, we encounter people for different purposes, once when we learn the lessons they offer, they may leave. And that's okay.

don't rely solely on human relationships

Don't build your entire world
around a single individual.
You'll end up disappointed.

People may come and go,
but Allah remains steadfast,
never leaving your side.

reality of kindness

Being kind means
that people
will sometimes
try to take
advantage of your
kindness.
Please do not let them
take away your light.
Know that your reward
is with Allah.

prioritizing our faith over worldly relationships

Sometimes we lose friends
that were really close to us.
What I've come to realize is that
if you strive to be a better Muslim,
sometimes some of our dear friends
are not really good for our deen,
and so Allah makes them disappear.
I know this may hurt you at the beginning,
but later you will see the goodness in it, inshAllah.
No one is worth
losing your akhirah over.

be bestowed with even greater blessings

I ask You, Allah,
to give
anyone
who might be jealous
of what You gave me,
more than I have.
Let them forget about me.

the transient nature of human relationships and the steadfastness of Allah's presence and love

Here's the thing with people –
you can ask them for help
and count on them.
But
sooner or later,
they will disappoint you,
somehow in some way,
/willingly or by accident/.
This is just how we are.
We are not perfect and
we tend to make a lot of mistakes.
And then there's God.
He's here,
every time,
all the time.
Even when He's the last one
you will ask for help,
He will still help you
and be there for you.

In the last couple of years, I've learned /or maybe I'm still learning/ that trusting people too much and expecting them to always be there for me is simply too much to ask for.

But… expecting & believing that Allah is ALWAYS here for you, this is where you won't ever end up disappointed.
This is the only relationship in our lives where you give LESS and still receive far more than you deserve.
Allah's love for us is a
NEVER-ENDING
one.

meaningful relationships

Friends who'll pray for you when you're gone,
family who'll pray for you as life moves on.
Surround yourself with those who'll remember you well, even
after you've departed and left.
Hold them close,
for their prayers and deeds
in your name,
may or will be your salvation
when needed most.

care and support

There are people
who silently cheer for you,
pray for you,
and support you from the sidelines.
They look after you
without your awareness.
Such individuals are rare to find,
and that's why they're invaluable.
Express gratitude to Allah for them
and strive to be that person for someone else.

V

MUSLIMAH

muminah / sister / hijab

This chapter is a lyrical exploration of the Muslimah's journey in Islam, highlighting her unwavering devotion, inner strength, and the modesty that defines her character.

clouded judgment

As a woman to another I want to urge you to be extremely cautious when choosing your spouse. It can be risky, especially if you're already in love before marriage.

Love has the ability to blind us at times, preventing us from seeing red flags that may be present and unfortunately, there could be many.

Seek advice from your parents as they can guide you and help you find a suitable spouse.

Sometimes, we are unable to see what's right in front of us, but our fathers would most likely recognize it immediately. They know us best and have a better understanding of what is truly good for us.

personal transformation

Being shy was never my thing before,
I was always loud and bold.
I wanted to attract attention from everyone
because I felt so lonely inside.
Today, I don't seek attention
from anyone anymore
I only seek to please my and your Lord.

defending the choice to wear a hijab

I'm the one who will decide
who shall see and who shall not see
my beauty.

Others have no right or say,
to determine my path, in any way.
I'll fight for my freedom of choice.
I'll fight for my rights.
I'll fight for my hijab.
Till the end of my life.

significant encounter with a woman wearing a hijab, the inspiration she provided, the bravery she exhibited

A few years ago when I went out for a walk, I met a woman wearing a hijab. I can't remember her face because I only saw her for a mere second, and I didn't dare to look for longer because I feared that she might feel uncomfortable.
I don't remember how old I was at that time, but I'm sure I was younger than 14 years old.
Little did I realize in that moment, that few years later, I would be like her. I could never imagine myself as a Muslim, but Allah had destined a different path for me. And little did she know how much she inspired me at that moment.
I never felt any hate towards Muslims in my heart. Instead, I regarded that courageous woman with admiration. How could she proudly wear the hijab in a world poised to judge her? And imagine, it was an era when there were not many hijabis in our town, and acceptance may not have flowed easily.
In that fleeting encounter, the woman inspired me. She ignited a spark in me, inspired me to be a little more me and to care a little less about what other people think about me.
This encounter serves as a reminder that we possess the power

to inspire, often unknowingly. Merely existing can touch the lives of others in profound ways.

I thank Allah for sending that woman into my life, even though it was only for 5 seconds; she gave me so much.

deep emotional impact

I didn't even realize how much
being covered
meant to me
until someone,
who was not supposed to,
saw me.
In that moment,
I wanted to disappear from this world.
My eyes were full of tears,
my heart clenched,
and I had no idea
how to erase a memory
of myself
without hijab
from that person's mind…
…stil regretting it.

finding liberation within the Islamic faith

If islam would oppress women,
I wouldn't become a Muslim
because more than anything,
I wanted freedom
and Islam is where I found it.

the positive aspects of hijab

Hijab became easy
when I realized how
beneficial it is.

journey of wearing a hijab

For all my sisters out there
struggling with hijab,
fighting for hijab,
wanting to wear a hijab…

You're strong and I believe you can overcome any hardship.
I know it's hard sometimes.
I know you get tired sometimes.
But keep going.
Keep fighting.
You'll get there.
You'll win this fight.
And the reward will absolutely be worth it.
Making duaa for you and sending you hugs!

don't compromise our values for acceptance

Take care of yourself, sister.
Allah set rules, some only for us, women.
Not to hold us back, not to oppress us,
but to protect us.
You're precious, don't try to fit in the society that won't accept you, not fully, until you bow down to what they idolize.
Allah set rules for us,
and those rules are actually freeing us,
providing us the freedom that we want so badly.
You must realize that while trying to fit in with others, you are actually oppressing yourself.

importance of modesty

Hide your beauty.
Hide it for the sake of your Creator.
Hide it for yourself.
Hide it for your protection
and
hide it for your safety.
I know getting attention from others because of your beauty might make you feel loved, but mostly it's not love it's just lust.
Don't allow yourself to be used.

inner qualities and meaningful connections

Even if you might think that showing your beauty and getting compliments for it will make you happy… trust me – it won't. Been there, done that.
Those few moments of adrenaline rush I got from male attention soon turned into emptiness.

proper hijab

Fix your hijab.
Fix it!
Did I sound harsh?
Did my words bother you?
Do you feel attacked?
No need to.
But
you still gotta fix it.
Not because of me,
certainly not because I said so.
Please don't ever do
anything to please others.
Just follow Allah's guidance
and Prophet's, sallallahu alejhi we sellem, sunnah,
that'll be enough.

This quote emphasizes the importance of adhering to the proper hijab as guided by Allah and the teachings of the Prophet Muhammad, sallallahu alejhi we sellem. It encourages individuals to ensure their hijab is in line with the Islamic principles, not because of external pressure or to please others, but for the sake of pleasing Allah. The quote acknowledges that the words may come across as firm but reassures the reader that there is no intention to attack or harm. It emphasizes that the intention is solely to remind and encourage adherence to the hijab for the sake of following Allah's guidance and the example set by the Prophet Muhammad, sallallahu alejhi we sellem. It encourages individuals to prioritize pleasing Allah rather than seeking validation or approval from others.

freedom

If you desire to liberate yourself
from the pressures
society places upon you,
the simplest path
to do it
is to follow
Allah's commands.
Then no one,
no force,
will ever succeed
in swaying you
towards actions
you'd rather not do.
Because having
a strong faith
will give you
Allah's
unconditional
protection and support.

VI

TRUST

tawakkul / yaqeen / rida
Through these poems, the poetry book encapsulates
the essence of trust as a cornerstone of Islamic faith,
inspiring readers to place their trust in Allah and find
comfort in His plan.

seeking His pleasure

I've learned that regardless of
what other people see and think
I should only care about
Allah's orders and whether
He is pleased.

the value of embracing sabr

We don't know qadr
but we can always have sabr.

personal empowerment and trust in Allah's plan

Don't let others decide for you;
accept a decision, take the necessary steps,
leave the rest to Allah,
and witness it unfold.

find comfort in Allah's knowledge and understanding

Just a gentle reminder,
- Allah knows.
Allah knows that what you're going through is hard.
He sees your pain,
and that alone should put you at ease.

even in difficult times, there are blessings to be found

You'll never find hardship
without a blessing in it.
That's how merciful
He is.

seek solace in prayer and trust Allah during difficult times

I know sometimes the pain
becomes overwhelming
It's okay,
just breathe,
calm down,
close your eyes,
let your tears
flow freely,
call upon Allah,
seek His help
ask for ease,
trust Him
and believe
that with every hardship,
comes ease.

redirect your prayers towards seeking what is ultimately beneficial for you in both the worldly life and the Hereafter

Sometimes we wish for things that Allah knows would not be good for us-
Trust Him
and instead of asking for something specific,
ask Him to grant you what's best for you
in this world and the next.

level of trust we place in Allah

Why do we worry so much
about what tomorrow holds?
Do we not trust our Creator
as much as we are claiming to?

rejections as a form of divine protection

I once read:
"Life's rejections are just
Allah's protections."
Imagine always having
this on our minds…
Life would be so much easier.
Let's try to remind ourselves
of this more often.
Trust Him.

Allah never leaves us empty-handed

Believe that your duaa
will be answered.
Do not fear that you
won't get what's best for you.

a positive outlook

Behind every delay in your life,
you will eventually see the goodness.
Learn to see Allah's protection
in the things you want but
do not get right away.

profound and beautiful outcome

How beautiful must be the reward
for those who remain patient
when times are hard.

limitless power and certainty that Alllah possesses

Self-doubt is
eating our dreams.
I don't understand
why we are doing this,
when Allah said:
"Be! And it is!" Qur'an 2:117

importance of obedience

"We hear and we obey."
It's as simple as that.
And you know what Allah said
about people who are like that?
"It is they who will ⌈truly⌉ succeed." (Qur'an 24:51)
I think this says more than enough.

surrender and acceptance of reality

I've tried numerous things and various methods
to succeed,
now, I'm taking a step back,
letting You take full control.
I understand that You've been the one
in control all along,
now, I'm just
finally, fully accepting it
and feeling comfortable
with it.
I'm releasing the control I thought I had
and finally placing my full trust in You!

tawakkul

Sometimes, you don't even
need any signs,
for it has been there
all along.
Just open your eyes,
and put your trust
in the One and Only,
believing He will do
what's best for you.

perfect timing

You can't compel
things to happen
as you wish.
Allah's timing is better anyway.
But you can compel yourself
to be patient
and at ease with His timing.

surrendering to His plans

Sometimes, all you need to do
is let go while placing full trust in Allah and His plans.
Everything will inevitably fall into
the exact place it belongs.

VII

HARAM

sinful / forbidden / impermissible
In this chapter of the poetry book, the verses touch
upon the boundary between what's allowed and
what's forbidden in Islam, capturing the struggle to
find spiritual purity.

it is not worth the damage

Haram relationships bring you more
heartbreak than happiness.
They slowly destroy your other relationship
without you even noticing it.
Haram relationships destroy your most
important relationship – the one with Allah.
Don't do that to yourself.
We already have enough sins,
enough to fix.
Don't,
because
it's
just
not
worth
it.

a result of engaging in haram relationship

I speak and write about this
because I have experienced it myself,
and I can see all the broken
hearts of my friends.
All the broken hearts
regretting it.
Love is something beautiful.
Love is something sacred.
Don't taint it with haram.

consequences

What did I see in haram relationships
apart from love?
- guilt
- feeling lost
- panic
- anxiety
- despair
- lost hope
- tears, lots of them
- loneliness
- tearing down
- wounds, deep ones
- feeling sorry
- wasted time

Now, it's up to you to decide – is that what you want?

break free

It's time for you to break free
from that haram relationship, you see.
I know it's hard,
I know it'll hurt,
I know tears may be shed,
I know.
But here's what I also know
- I know who can save you.
I know Who holds the power to save you.
It is the One and Only – Allah.
The One Who created everything,
including you.
He alone can aid you through this test.
He is the only one who can help you
get better, no matter
the hardship.
Turn to Him,
with trust and belief,
pour out your heart,
find solace in grief.
For the Only One who can truly mend
your broken heart

is the One who
crafted it.

prohibition serves as a means of protection

You may wonder why,
why is this all happening to me?
What did I do to deserve this?
Why does it hurt so much?
I simply fell in love…
I understand my dear,
I understand.
I'm sorry
but I must be
brutally
honest
with you for a moment.
Have you ever considered
why Allah has prohibited
relationships before marriage?
It is to save us from this,
it is to save us from heartbreak's abyss.
If only we'd listened…
If only we'd follow His guidance and decree…
If only we'd obey…
What do you think would be?

PROHIBITION SERVES AS A MEANS OF PROTECTION

If you believe haram can bring you
everlasting joy & happiness,
you're mistaken.
Whenever
I engaged in something haram
I would found myself
collapsed on the floor,
broken-hearted,
begging for forgiveness
&
ease.
But
on the contrary,
I have never, ever
found myself
unhappy
while fulfilling what Allah has commanded me to do.

burden

Sins will
suffocate you
in every
possible way.

remorse and guilt

Regretting our sins
is actually a blessing.
Because how far from Allah you must be
if you don't feel even slightest hint of regret
after
sinning?

the significance of striving for righteousness

Sinning only brought forth the worst
feelings within me…
Guilt, shame & sadness.

impact of sins

Sins are like poison
to your imaan.

Allah's judgment

Why do we fear that people will
uncover our deepest & darkest secrets
when Allah already knows every detail…

regret

Zina may provide you moments of pleasure
but it will serve you a lifetime of regret.

the consequences of engaging in haram actions and the negative outcomes they can lead to

Whatever haram you're in
it will always end the same.
Haram leads only to
heartbreak.

longing and vulnerability; surrender and emotional turmoil

Down on my
knees again,
tears escaping
my eyes,
my heart
is breaking.
All I want is to feel the
nearness of Him.

tranquility

If you're not praying,
yet still feel at ease,
you should be concerned
for yourself…
That ease is a trap,
a calm before the storm.

manipulating the boundaries of halal

Be careful
of people who try
to convince themselves
that haram can be halal.
Be careful
of people who try
to beautify haram
and make it seem halal.
Haram never was
and never will be halal.

self-control and discipline

If you can abstain from food for almost whole day
for 30 full days,
you can also restrain from everything else
that is harmful or detrimental to you.
This means that you have the capacity
to cultivate and maintain any good habit,
demonstrating discipline and achieving your goals,
and that you can achieve anything you want,
if Allah wills.

the long-term consequences

Staying away
from haram
might be hard,
but
spending your
eternity
in Jahannam
is definitely harder.

genuine concern

I beg you,
as your sister in Islam,
who wants to see you in Jannah,
I beg you,
please stay away from haram.
Some things are easier said than done
but it's your eternity in question.
Where do you want to end up?

staying true to the teachings of the faith

Please don't allow yourself
to be one of those who try to
modernize Islam.
Don't try to make halal
something that is haram.

protective shield

If you ensure your imaan is high,
you'll shield yourself from sinning.
Each transgression appears more obscene,
when your imaan is steadfast and keen.

stay alert

Satan won't immediately deter you
from praying, that's clear,
at first, he takes small steps,
starting with things that may not appear severe.
But don't be fooled; those small steps, they matter,
for small sins can lead to bigger ones, more complex.
It could happen to anyone, quickly and discreetly,
beware and stay vigilant,
don't let Satan lead you astray.

heartfelt prayer

Ya Allah,
please,
grant me
the strength
to resist
worldly
temptations.
Allahumme ameen!

remorse

I've lost so many pieces of myself
because of my sins.
I'm uncertain if there's
any of me remaining...
Allah's mercy is vast, and the opportunity for forgiveness and spiritual renewal is always available to those who genuinely seek it. It's never too late to turn back to Allah, seek His forgiveness, and rebuild a sense of self through faith and righteous actions.

priorities

I'm letting go of my beloved
because it's clear
that I momentarily prioritized him
over Allah.
And I can't expect a
happy ending if
Allah's pleasure isn't
my primary focus.
#HaramRelationships

the void within one's soul

The emptiness inside you
cannot be filled
with the haram,
not in the long run.
Your soul
is yearning
for closeness
with its Creator.
Give your soul
what it truly needs,
and you'll transform your whole life
for the better.
With His help.

VIII

REPENTANCE

tawbah / istighfar / mercy

Through these poems, the poetry book embodies the essence of repentance as a way to cleanse the heart and renew the connection with Allah in the Islamic tradition.

pure hearts

It's important to cleanse
our hearts on a daily basis.
Repent every day
and every night.
Ask Allah for forgiveness
and don't forget
- He loves those who repent.

repentance becomes a lifeline

I feel as though I've lost a piece of myself
every time I've committed a sin.
At some point I was forced to stop
otherwise I would lose all pieces of me.
Repenting and seeking forgiveness was me
preventing myself from drowning.
Allah granted us the chance to repent
and for that, I am truly grateful.

emotional aftermath

I wish I could have more control over myself
in the moments before committing a sin.
Then, I wouldn't have to weep in despair
as I lay in bed, pondering my chance for repair.

clash between the shame and guilt

I feel ashamed to ask for forgiveness
because I was so shameless while committing a sin.
I know it is misguided to feel this way,
but sometimes I question my worthiness, doubting
if I am deserving of
His forgiveness.
And then there comes the beauty of His
when He says: ask & I'll forgive.*
*Say, "O My servants who have transgressed against themselves [by sinning], do not despair of the mercy of Allāh. Indeed, Allāh forgives all sins. Indeed, it is He who is the Forgiving, the Merciful."
   Qur'an 39:53

recognizing one's worth and avoiding self-pity

"There are many who are better than me."
 "I'm unworthy of His forgiveness."
Listen to my words!
Apologies for the blunt truth,
but you're swimming
in a pool of self-pity.
Get out or else you'll drown.
Allah would never have guided you
to Islam in the first place
if He did not deem you worthy.
He would not have led you here
if He didn't want to forgive.
Stop
swimming
in
a
pool
of
self-pity!

the tendency of humanity to be impatient and seek immediate fulfillment

"Allah is truly with those who are patient." Qur'an 2:153
Yet, humanity remains blinded,
seeking everything and seeking it now.

the mercy and forgiveness of Allah

What leads you to believe
that Allah won't forgive
when in the Qur'an, He declared:
"...for I am the Acceptor of Repentance,
Most Merciful."
　Qur'an 2:160

satan's deceitful whispers and manipulative intentions

There are many ways to make bad deeds
disappear and vanish,
yet Satan continues to try
to convince you that you're too bad
to stand in front of Allah…
Don't fall into that trap,
Satan is full of deceit.
Can't you see that
he just wants you in
Jahannam with him?

let go

Forgive yourself for your past sins,
Allah has already forgiven.

plea for forgiveness

I'm sorry Ya Rabb,
please forgive me,
forgive me
for
falling into the same trap
all over again
and again
and again.
I'm sorry Ya Rabb,
please forgive me,
forgive me
because
I keep repeating the same mistakes
all over again
and again
and again.
I'm sorry Ya Rabb,
please forgive me,
forgive me
for
disappointing you
all over again

and again
and again.
I'm
sorry
Ya
Rabb,
please
forgive
me,
forgive
me,
all
over
again
and
again
and
again.

shortcomings in repentance

Ya Rabbi,
please forgive me
for all the sins committed
and forgotten.
I acknowledge that there's a possibility
that I may have forgotten to repent
for some of these sins.
I'm asking for Your forgiveness
for all that I've overlooked and not repented for.

virtue of forgiveness

Being able
to forgive
those who have wronged you
is one of the greatest things
Allah has bestowed upon you,
because it grants you a peaceful mind,
while those who wronged you
will have to confront their deeds
on the Day of Judgment
if they don't repent in time.

IX

CHANGE

muhasabah / ihsan / nashat

depth of commitment to my faith

I want everybody to know my story
yet not necessarily my name.
I want them to comprehend who I was
before Islam graced my life.
For only then will they understand
why I clutch onto my belief so steadfastly
- because I yearn to truly live.

it is okay

It's okay.
It's okay if they don't understand
the lifestyle you have chosen to live.
It's okay if they think you're strange.
It's okay if they no longer like you.
It's okay if they judge you.
It's okay if they speak ill of you.
It is
okay.
As long as you have faith,
as long as you trust in Allah,
as long as you obey Him,
as long as He comes first.
It's okay
and it will always be okay.
Because you're the one with hope for Jannah,
while those people have nothing but this Dunya.
They are and will remain miserable.
It is
okay.

freedom to change

You are allowed to change your mind.
You are allowed to change your opinion.
You are allowed to change how you feel.
You are allowed to change.
Don't worry about their words.
If Allah has guided you, don't worry about your past.
Put your effort & focus on the future, and become the best version of yourself.
You are allowed to change.

Allah does not hold your past against you

We all grow and change.
Two years, two months, two weeks or even two days ago, you could have been a completely different person, living a different life.
Perhaps you were not the best example, but guess what? Allah does not care about who you were & what you did. If you sincerely repent and seek forgiveness, He will forgive. There is no doubt in it.
So do not let your past scare and discourage you
from becoming a better person and better Muslim.
We all started at the bottom,
so don't worry.
Just make the move,
start with small things,
step by step,
Allah will help!

focus on the present and future rather than dwelling on the past

Don't despair about what was,
for it's already done and gone.
Worry about who you are today,
and care about tomorrow.
Your sins reside in the past,
which you cannot change,
but you can strive to obey
Allah today and never stop
asking for forgiveness.

the tendency to modify our behavior based on who is observing us

When you're being observed
by someone significant,
your behavior alters accordingly.
When you're in the company of friends,
your demeanor takes on a different shape.
When you're alone, often you pay no heed
to your actions and conduct,
for there appears to be no audience...
Yet, oh, why, do we consistently neglect
the fact that Allah witnesses all?
Why do we not prioritize our concern?

find a hidden message in this one

Even on the rock bottom
of the sea,
you can find beauty:
pearls.
Collect them,
and return
richer than you
were before.

A hidden message can be interpreted as an encouragement to find beauty and value even in the most challenging and difficult circumstances. The metaphor of being at the rock bottom of the sea signifies a state of despair or adversity. However, the mention of pearls symbolizes the potential for finding treasures amidst adversity.

The hidden message suggests that when faced with hardships, rather than succumbing to despair, one should search for the hidden pearls of wisdom, growth, and beauty within those experiences. by collecting and embracing these pearls, one can emerge from difficult situations richer in wisdom, resilience, and personal growth.

challenges faced by reverts

The struggle of reverts can truly humble us
in so many ways.
They hide from their relatives
the one thing that brings them happiness,
and they seek every possible way to pray.
Hoping no one enters the room while they're praying,
girls pray in improvised hijabs because they can't afford to buy
one just yet, as their parents may disapprove if discovered.
Yet, when they reflect on their journey, they remain grateful
for all the difficulties, for through their struggles, they draw
closer to Allah.
They sought every possible way to pray,
while we delay
until the last possible minute to stay away...

hope and encouragement

We all started at the rock bottom,
and you honestly do not want to know
from where I came and who I was
before Allah guided me.
But that is not important anymore.
If in your heart
the desire to follow
His path is born,
do not listen to Satan
who will try to convince you
that you're not good enough.
Allah will look beyond your imperfections,
and He will look beyond your sins.
Those things are truly not important to Him.
As long as you repent
and distance yourself from old habits,
you are good to go.
Trust me, we've all been there.

growth and development

I know some things aren't
easy to practice, easy to accept...
But please, oh please,
strive to be better
each and every day,
strive to be as good as you can be,
strive to be the best version of yourself.

the power of prayer

Sometimes you are only
one prayer away
from changing &
overturning your life.

new perspective

All my life, I have fought
with feelings of being
unwanted & unworthy.
However, it was later,
when I converted
to Islam, that I began to
believe in and see myself
as someone who is more than enough.
Allah has bestowed upon me
abundant blessing,
and one of the things that has
helped me through this journey
is the realization that
Allah deemed me worthy.
He saw me fit to be guided,
so how could I still feel unwanted
when He guided me and granted me
'new life' – life as Muslimah.
Wanted. Worthy. Enough.

responsibilities

No one will strive for you,
to make you a better Muslim.
This is a journey you must pursue alone,
to fortify your faith on your own.

powerful

I am brave, you see,
I know some people find it hard
to think highly about themselves,
I, too, am one of them.
So let me say this loud and clear
I am brave because
only Allah and I are aware of the immense courage I had to summon to choose and tread this path that I am currently walking.
I acknowledge my bravery,
but I always remember where this strength originates and who bestowed it upon me.
Everything I am is a result of Allah's inspiration,
and I am proud of myself.

grow

If you don't pray at all
begin with praying fard.
If you pray fard
add sunnah prayer.
If you pray the sunnah prayers,
include the night prayer.
If you pray the night prayer
add the morning and evening dhikr.
Always strive to better yourself,
and always seek new ways to improve.
Growth is necessary to
reach our ultimate destination, which is Jannah.
Don't remain stagnant in the same place
throughout your life; aim for growth.

X

GRATITUDE

shukr / alhamdulillah / sadaqah

The verses in this section serve as a poetic reminder of the significance of gratitude in Islamic teachings, urging individuals to express thankfulness in their daily lives and spiritual journey.

pause and engage in a moment, express gratitude

Have we thanked Allah today
for everything He gave us?
Stop reading and
DO IT right now!

gratitude and humility before Allah

Whatever we possess is from Allah.
Even with lifetime of worship we cannot
sufficiently thank Him.
No amount of good deeds alone can grant
us entry to Jannah without His boundless mercy.
He gave us so much that even if we were to give
our all, it would still fall short.
But that should never discourage us from trying,
for therein lies the beauty.

positive transformation

You've changed.
I know,
and I thank Allah
every day for it.

generosity and selflessness

I see
people who have nothing
give their everything
for His sake
and in the end
they are the ones
who gain and have
more than anyone.

power of gratitude

If we would ever start
counting our blessings,
the problems we have
would become insignificant.
Alhamdulillah

kept between oneself and Allah

May your most beautiful moments stay hidden,
hidden from people.
May only Allah know what makes your soul happy and what
makes your heart smile.

balanced mindset

When you are experiencing
good days, be thankful
&
when you are facing
challenging days, be patient.
Shukr
&
sabr.

seemingly minor actions may hold great value

In Islam, nothing goes to waste,
you earn rewards even while you sleep,
when you smile at a stranger you meet,
or clean a path to make it neat,
Even the smallest acts hold weight,
and who knows,
perhaps these little deeds we sow,
will be what saves us
on the Day of Judgment, so,
remember, nothing goes to waste,
not even the smallest things.

the ultimate source of everything

What you have to realize is that
everything comes from Him.
You're successful
because you're intelligent,
but your knowledge
comes from Allah.
You're praised
for your appearance,
but your beauty
is a gift from Allah.
It all originates and returns
from Him to Him.
It's never about you,
and it's always about Him.
Staying humble,
it is.

XI

HEREAFTER

Akhirah / Jannah / Jahannam
The verses in this section provide a poetic glimpse into the Islamic belief in the Hereafter, emphasizing the importance of living a life that leads to success in the afterlife.

detachment

Sometimes, letting go of this world
will bring nothing but the best
in the next one.

making the most of each moment

How beautiful it is that during Ramadan, we are cautious about wasting time because we understand the value of every moment. We constantly fear that it might be our last, so we strive to make the most of it.

Indeed, this is beautiful, but let's not forget that this is how we should act and think every single day.
Sometimes, the distractions of this worldly life make us forget that there is no promised tomorrow. Each day could be our last. This is the harsh reality of our existence.
I understand that some people may not like to be reminded of death & it can be challenging to think about it all the time. However as Muslims, it is essential for us. We must remind ourselves & others about death frequently. This way, we will always think twice before wasting time & engaging in sinful acts, not only during Ramadan.
Our time in this world is limited.
Utilize every possible moment to worship
your Creator.
One day, you will be gone, and among the few things that will remain are your good deeds.
They will shield you from punishment in the Hellfire and you

will enjoy eternity in Jannah.
Don't waste your time,
worship Allah!

true fulfillment lie in the hereafter

Running after this Dunya is pointless,
Allah has already told us:
"And the next life is certainly far better for you than this one."
   Qur'an 93:4

crucial decisions

At some point, you have to
accept an important decision,
either to be occupied with this Dunya
or to follow Allah's orders.
You really can't have both.
It's either Jannah or Jahannam
   - you choose.

confront the topic of death and be mindful of it

People often shy away
from discussing the topic of death,
but I don't mind addressing it,
for it is something that will catch
us all sometime.
Remind yourself of its presence often.
Today you're here,
tomorrow you're nowhere near.
Ask yourself if you've done enough,
and if you're prepared
to meet Allah.

the temporary attractions of this worldly life

This Dunya might be appealing,
but it's merely because you haven't glimpsed
into Jannah yet.

importance of effort

If you want to win,
you have to put some effort in.
A reward cannot be claimed,
if worthiness is not attained.
You can't get into Jannah
without being tested first.

striving for excellence in one's actions and deeds

This life is a test
so make sure your
score is the best.

the fleeting nature of worldly desires and everlasting joy and bliss in Jannah

Don't lose Jannah for temporary pleasures that this world is offering you. Delights of this worldly life are fleeting and transitory, but Jannah is not.
Remember that true and eternal enjoyment awaits the believers in Jannah.

never ultimately defeated

Believers are never at loss,
and
there are no sad endings for them.

pursuing worldly perfection is ultimately futile, as it is unattainable

Striving for perfection
in this world is
pointless
since we already
know
we can't achieve it.
Jannah is promised to be perfect
yet we waste so much time on
this Dunya that could never be.

worldly pursuits and possession

Every single thing on this world
will be worthless in the end.
Every single thing we own,
we will attempt to trade for something far greater.
We run around,
trying to make the most out of this world,
seeking optimal living conditions.
Yet, in doing so, we often forget
that eventually, we will have to leave
all of that behind us.
What will endure
are our deeds,
the good ones
and
the bad ones.
In the end, it won't matter how much we possessed,
but rather who we are and what good we left behind.
Are we prepared for that?

profound admiration and love

I honestly cannot wait
to meet
Prophet Muhammad, sallallahu alejhi we sellem.

rewards promised in Jannah

Our happiness will truly begin when we enter Jannah.

preserve and find strength

When struggling,
remind yourself
that at the end of the road
Jannah is waiting for you.

longing

Just wait a little longer,
we will be home soon, by Allah's mercy.
Jannah.

appreciation for the present moment

Your time here
is limited.
Let that sink in.

the trap of procrastination and underestimation of the limited time we have in this life

Our days are numbered.
Every day we are closer
to leaving this world behind.
Please make sure that
you are as prepared
as you can be.
Don't let Satan
delude you into
thinking that you have
enough time,
because in reality
- you don't.

the importance of continuous self-improvement

Strive to be better every day,
for how else
can we become
those
who deserve
to enter Jannah?

deep concern for your non-Muslim family members

I was just reading about Jahannam,
at first, my heart broke for myself,
because I know I have many shortcomings...
But then I started to think about my non-Muslim family.
I read about all the terrible consequences for those who worship other than Allah, and not a single person in my family is Muslim.
And my heart continues to break for them...
Ya Allah, guide them all,
they are lost without Your guidance,
and they will suffer eternally without Your Mercy.
It's important to remember that while we may have concerns for the spiritual well-being of our family and friends, Allah's wisdom and mercy are vast. Islamic teachings emphasize the importance of prayer and inviting others to Islam through good character and example. Continue to make sincere supplications for their guidance and be a source of positive influence in their lives. Ultimately, the decision to embrace Islam is a personal one, and your prayers may play a part in their spiritual journey.

no way to escape

Indeed, there is no surviving the Hell,
there's no coming out, no escape,
there's no end once you're there.
So, while we have the chance, while we're here,
let's ensure we never reach there,
through our faith, deeds, and sincere prayer.

wise choices

Jannah is forever,
but so is Jahannam…
Choose your forever wisely.
It's up to you, your decisions, and your actions.
It's up to you,
you're the one choosing your final destination.

keep your focus on what is eternal and of greater significance

Don't allow your love for the Dunya,
to surpass your love for the Akhirah.

focus where it matters

If your primary concern is the Akhirah,
the whole world will try to follow you
and the best part is
– you won't even care about it.

charity

Whatever you give
in the name of Allah
is never lost,
it always comes back to you
in one way or another.

be mindful

If we can barely withstand
the physical fires of this world,
why are we so heedless
of the more dreadful and eternal fire that awaits?

forgetful species are we

We are unprepared for
what is yet to come,
and so fond of wasting
our precious time,
not even realizing how
limited it is.
We spend hours on
things that hold no value
on the Day of Judgment.
We run towards haram
and away from halal.
We find the good to difficult,
and the bad is too easy.
Forgetful species are we.

AFTERWORD

Dear Reader,

Thank you so much for investing your time in reading my first published book!

This book holds a special place in my heart, and I am truly grateful that you decided to give it a chance. Writing a book has been a dream of mine since I was 12 years old, and the fact that it has materialized into a collection of poems and quotes about Islam is beyond what I could have imagined. Yet, I believe it was all written for me and for you to read this book, guided by none other than Allah.

I sincerely hope you enjoyed reading this book and that you gained some new knowledge. My aspiration is that my words have left a positive impact on you and your faith. May this book be a source of goodness, both in this life and the hereafter, for both you and me.

If you found joy in this book, I would be delighted to hear your thoughts about it. Please feel free to reach out and share your reflections. You can connect with me on Instagram or TikTok – @HannaTheWriter. Additionally, if you believe someone else could benefit from this book, do share it. Let's gain some good deeds together, shall we?

Thank you once again for being part of this journey.

Warm regards,

   Hanna K. Brojan

Made in the USA
Columbia, SC
22 January 2025